Praise for *The Beginner's Guide to Karma*

"The book's short chapters allow for a quick read, but readers can also elect to take their time by using the end-of-chapter exercises to focus on inner peace and building good karma. To that end, the authors include useful meditations, examples of virtuous and nonvirtuous acts, and visualizations in appendices. A short but detailed introduction that may inspire readers to set out on a karmic journey."

— *Kirkus Reviews*

"Karma is an important philosophical principle that describes how the complex nature of cause and effect works as the engine of life. It is also a household word embraced by popular culture. *The Beginner's Guide to Karma* succinctly explains karma in language that is clear and practical. It will help everyone understand this ancient wisdom and how to apply it to bring more positivity to their life."

— Anam Thubten, author of *The Magic of Awareness* and *No Self, No Problem*

T0315438

THE BEGINNER'S GUIDE TO

KARMA

Also by Lama Lhanang Rinpoche
and Mordy Levine

The Tibetan Book of the Dead for Beginners:
A Guide to Living and Dying

THE BEGINNER'S GUIDE TO

KARMA

How to Live with Less Negativity and More Peace

LAMA LHANANG RINPOCHE
& MORDY LEVINE

New World Library
Novato, California

New World Library
14 Pamaron Way
Novato, California 94949

Text design by Tona Pearce Myers

Library of Congress Cataloging-in-Publication Data

Names: Lama Lhanang, Rinpoche, author. | Levine, Mordy, author.
Title: The beginner's guide to karma : how to live with less negativity and more
    peace / Lama Lhanang Rinpoche & Mordy Levine.
Description: Novato, California : New World Library, [2024] | Includes bibli-
    ographical references. | Summary: "In *The Beginner's Guide to Karma*, two
    practitioners of Tibetan Buddhism unravel the complexities of karma, an
    idea widely known but little understood in the modern West"-- Provided
    by publisher.
Identifiers: LCCN 2024021430 (print) | LCCN 2024021431 (ebook) | ISBN
    9781608688722 (paperback) | ISBN 9781608688739 (epub)
Subjects: LCSH: Karma.
Classification: LCC BL2015.K3 L36 2024 (print) | LCC BL2015.K3 (ebook) |
    DDC 294.5/22--dc23/eng/20240718
LC record available at https://lccn.loc.gov/2024021430
LC ebook record available at https://lccn.loc.gov/2024021431

First printing, October 2024
ISBN 978-1-60868-872-2
Ebook ISBN 978-1-60868-873-9

Printed in Canada

10   9   8   7   6   5   4   3   2   1

Dedication of Merit

May the teachings in this book reduce suffering.
May the teachings in this book reduce confusion.
May the teachings in this book bring joy and liberation.
We dedicate these merits to the enlightenment
of all sentient beings.

Mind precedes all mental states. Mind is their chief; they are all mind-wrought. If with an impure mind a person speaks or acts, suffering follows him like the wheel that follows the foot of the ox.

Mind precedes all mental states. Mind is their chief; they are all mind-wrought. If with a pure mind a person speaks or acts, happiness follows him like his never-departing shadow.

— BUDDHA, DHAMMAPADA

Accept life and enjoy every moment.
Don't use the poisons, they destroy our life.
Ignorance creates confusion.
Anger creates hatred and jealousy.
Jealousy creates anger and hatred.
Grasping and greed create attachment and being
    unsatisfied.
Always stay on the dharma path.

— LAMA LHANANG RINPOCHE

Contents

Preface

As we write these words, we can't imagine a time where greater divisiveness existed in this country and around the world. There are many issues that divide humanity. It truly feels like the world is on fire.

Unfortunately, our differences pervade every aspect of our lives. Neighbors, family members, and longtime friends are now at odds with one another. Although humanity rarely agrees on any important issue, the degree of extremism seems to be at an all-time high. The lack of tolerance — on both sides — has been examined extensively in media, academia, the workplace, social media, and conversations among friends and family members.

It is not that we disagree that is the problem. It is *how* we disagree. Historians point to various moments in human history where we have fought bitterly among ourselves. All involved experienced great loss and suffering. This appears to be the path we are on now.

What's karma got to do with it? Everything.

Prior to the Buddha's teachings, the concept of karma was mechanistic, transactional, and ritualistic. If you wanted good weather for your crops, you would perform an animal sacrifice ritual. If the weather was good, the sacrifice worked. If not, the priest would promise good weather in the future.

The Buddha's contribution to the understanding and development of karma was significant. His enlightened mind was able to refine and expand the teachings of karma to show that we can stop our perpetuation of negative actions. He taught that karma is far more sophisticated than the simple, linear cause and effect most of us think of. And finally, as we will see in chapter 2, the Buddha taught that intention or motivation is the basis for karma. It is not a mechanistic action.

In this book, we do our best to adhere to the Buddha's teachings on karma, and not just because we are Buddhists. We consider the Buddha's teachings on karma to be the most accurate explanation of how the world works. Our intention is to give readers a map on how to proceed with less negativity, greater compassion, more open-mindedness, and ultimately greater peace toward others. This naturally leads to tranquility and liberation.

Understanding how karma works for individuals will help us all understand our role in the current environment. None of us got here by happenstance. We are all part of the problem, and therefore we all need to be part of the solution.

By implementing this knowledge in the current climate, we can release the psychological and emotional pressures that continue to worsen the lives of our friends, colleagues, neighbors, and all other sentient beings. Understanding how we got here allows us to change our direction. Learning about karma will help us understand why we are experiencing this contentiousness so broadly and deeply. But more important, understanding karma will allow us to reduce anger and division among ourselves, our community, our country, and the world.

Lama Lhanang always teaches that "peace starts in your heart." Creating positive karma starts there too.

CHAPTER 1

What Is Karma?

The concept of karma predated the birth of Gautama Buddha some 2,600 years ago. Karma was first mentioned in the Upanishads, which are some of the oldest writings from the early days of Hindu thought, several hundred years before the Buddha's life. In addition to Hinduism and Buddhism, many other Eastern religions believe in the core principles of karma, including Jainism, Sikhism, Shintoism, and Taoism.

Karma is a Sanskrit word that means "action." In our use of the term, it refers to both the action and its consequences. While *action* usually implies physical movement, in the case of karma it refers to the actions of physical movement, speech, or thought. By acting, speaking, or thinking, we create karma.

What are the consequences of our actions of body, speech, or mind?

- We are likely to repeat our habits.
- We are likely to find ourselves in an environment where the behavior is common.
- We are likely to be the recipient of the actions we take.

Here is an example. If you get anxious whenever you receive your monthly bills in the mail, the following may happen:

1. You will be anxious whenever the mail comes at the end of the month.
2. You will find yourself in an environment that triggers that anxiety.
3. Those around you will be uneasy in your presence, especially when you are anxious, triggering more anxiety in you.

Our reactions — in the form of thought, speech, or action — create karma.

Attributes That Describe Karma

Karma is also known as the law of cause and effect. What we do, how we speak, and what we think (cause) affects ourselves and others (effect).

We all know about the law of gravity. You don't have to be a physicist to see or experience it. We may not be able to explain how gravity works, but we know from direct experience that it is a fact of life.

Karma is similar. Although there are few masters who can explain its intricacies, we can see it at work in our lives when we learn to pay attention and know what to look for.

In the Majjhima Nikāya, the Buddha describes karma as follows: "When this exists, that comes to be; with the arising of this, that arises. When this does not exist, that does not come to be; with the cessation of this, that ceases."

In our personal ethical world, karma is the operating principle. Nothing happens without a preceding cause. That is a fact. We may not be able to control the weather or certain biological events; but when we understand the cause-and-effect nature of karma, we can determine how we live and experience our lives going forward.

Another attribute of karma is that the impact of our actions may be greater than the original action taken. Karma is referred to as a seed that gestates in our mind, which is an appropriate analogy. For example, seeds grow and the resulting plant becomes much larger than the original seed. In fact, over time one seed can populate an entire field of roses or weeds!

We may take a small action and think nothing of it. However, the consequences can be far greater than intended or expected.

- You drive to the grocery store, which is just around the corner, telling yourself it's just a short ride. You don't wear your seat belt. You get into an accident that destroys your car and results in physical injuries for you and your passengers.

- You give ten dollars for food to a person experiencing homelessness. Although it may seem like a small gesture, it could enable that individual to turn their life around. As a result of that seemingly small charitable act, along with other causes at play, a few weeks later that individual may be living with a roof over their head and working again. A small act can have a great impact.

For more glaring examples, many wars have been fought and thousands killed when the leaders of two countries disagree. How can a small act have such large consequences? Karmic actions (seeds) are planted in our consciousness and interact with the play of the universe. As the seeds mature, they are fertilized by the myriad karmic actions and connections that interact with them.

Another aspect of karma is related cause and effect. If you don't do something, you don't create karma. When you plant an apple seed, you expect the tree that grows to bear apples. When you don't grow an apple tree, don't expect apples. If you want the result, you must do the work. If you don't want the result, don't take the action that may cause the result. Although it sounds obvious, it's an important attribute of karma.

His Holiness the Fourteenth Dalai Lama reflects this attribute when he talks about creating peace: "Peace does not come through prayer, we human beings must create peace." He is even more direct when he says, "Problems created by human beings have to be solved by human beings."

Karma is also definite. Our actions have concrete effects. We may not know how, where, when, or to what degree, but karmic actions definitely produce results. Karma does not lie, and we can't run away from it. Whether our karmic actions are negative or positive, their effects will ensue. As the great Hindu Christian saint Paramahansa Yogananda said, "Before you act, you have freedom, but after you act, the effect of that action will follow you whether you want it to or not. That is the law of karma."

Does karma mean our lives are predetermined? No, it does not imply fate or predetermination. In fact, just the opposite. We determine our future by exercising our free will. We decide how we think, speak, and act.

We cannot predict our future with great specificity. But we know that creating positive karma will liberate our minds with each passing day. Negative karma, on the other hand, leads to anger, anxiety, fear, irritation, jealousy, annoyance, and numerous other afflictions.

Tibetan Buddhism offers "antidotes" — meditation practices, visualizations, behaviors — we can apply to purify negative karma. In chapter 8, we will review the different methods available to mitigate the effects of the karma we have created, including purification, transference, and dilution.

By doing these practices, we learn to change our current and future behavior to avoid habituating our triggered reactions. We start to see what options are at our disposal and which actions may yield negative or positive results.

It's one thing to learn how to heal your finger after you hit it with a hammer. It's even better to learn how not to hit your finger at all. If you know that anger causes harm to yourself and others, after the fact you can purify anger's karmic effects. But better yet, over time we learn to be angry less often and with less intensity.

Our present situation and state of mind result from our past thoughts, speech, and actions. How we act, speak, or think at this moment, in reaction to our current circumstances, determines our experience in the next moment. How we live today affects how we live tomorrow, the next day, next week, next month, and next year. Right now, we are creating our own future through our karma!

Triggers and Habits

Looking at the moments prior to our actions, we can identify triggers that seem to cause our behavior. But are they really the cause? If so, one might place the blame on those triggers. We will find out shortly who is responsible.

What happens when these triggers appear again and again? Our behavioral response becomes a pattern or habit. Habits can be good or bad. Let's look at a few.

- It was my third divorce. Why can't I keep a spouse? They are always angry with me.
- My boss keeps getting on my case when I'm late. He says others are starting to come late too.
- Every time I go to that buffet restaurant I eat too much and have trouble sleeping. It keeps me and my husband up all night.
- My car broke down again. Now we can't afford that vacation.
- I am tired of looking for my keys. I get angry and it makes me late.
- I lose my temper whenever he talks to me in that tone of voice. It takes me hours to calm down.
- I always get anxious when my bills come. I must juggle my budget to make ends meet.

- Why am I nervous before I travel? I can't sleep for days before I get on the plane.
- Why do I always feel anxious when my phone dings? It's as if I always expect bad news. And then I'm on edge when I respond.
- When I smile on my walk to work, I notice that others smile back. I'm in a better mood for the rest of the day.
- I am always on time with my work projects, so my boss keeps giving me more responsibility. Now I just got a promotion!
- When I started to eat only healthy foods, it became easier to eat that way. Now I feel better, and my family eats healthier too.
- I call my father every week to say hello. Now my son calls me each week to check in. I am not so lonely when he calls.

What do these examples have in common?

- They are all actions of physical movement, speech, and/or thought.
- They are all reactions triggered by a preceding thought or external action.

- There is a consequence for the person doing the action. In most cases, those consequences affect family, friends, and colleagues.
- The reactions described are perpetuated again and again. They have become habits.

Wouldn't it be great if we could eliminate our negative habits and states of mind, and perpetuate those that serve us well? Can we use these habits to our advantage and learn from them? Absolutely yes. Let's take the next step and see how or what is responsible for these reactions.

Who Is Responsible?

According to the Buddha, "I am the owner of my actions, heir to my actions, born of my actions, related through my actions, and have my actions as my arbitrator. Whatever I do, for good or for evil, to that I will fall heir."

We may not be able to prevent what happens to us because of another individual or circumstance. Our circumstances are determined by the results of our past karmic actions and the karmic actions of others we're interacting with. However, *we can control how we respond to any situation that arises* — pleasant or unpleasant. We can control how we think, act, and speak. When you think about it, that is the only thing we really can control.

We are 100 percent responsible for our own state of mind. Only you can make yourself happy or mad. You may be triggered by someone or something — or even your own thought! But you can decide how you feel and respond. If we act skillfully, we create positive karma. If we act unskillfully, we continue to propagate negative karma.

Because we have the ability (with practice) to choose how we act in response to circumstances, we can break the habits we have been perpetuating until now. How? We stop our habitual reactions. But as we know, when we are triggered, under stress, in the heat of the moment, we find ourselves repeating previous behaviors, reacting unskillfully.

Mindfulness is the key to seeing the reactive thoughts develop in our minds. As the Buddha taught, our actions are preceded by thought, so we need to know what is in our minds. Once we see the beginnings of anger or irritation, we can apply the appropriate remedy so the negative habit does not continue.

In chapter 5, we will discuss how to recognize habits so we can eliminate them at their root. In chapter 6, we will go into detail on the tools available to break these habits and create positive karma.

Everybody has the potential to be free of negative states of mind. And everyone has the potential to be a Buddha, a Mother Teresa, or a Gandhi. The time to start is now. If we don't, our habits will only continue and strengthen.

EXERCISE

Identify one action you took today (of body, speech, or mind). Can you remember your thoughts or state of mind that preceded it?

CHAPTER 2

What Makes Karma Heavy or Light?

From a karmic perspective, what is the difference between getting angry at a loved one and getting angry after watching a politician on TV that you dislike? You unintentionally killed an insect while driving today. What is your karma? What is the difference between killing an ant and killing a human? If you think the karmic effects should be different in these cases, you are right.

Heavy karma means the consequence will be serious and have a larger impact on you and others. Light karma means the consequences will be lighter. Let's examine some reactions that we experience in our lives. Can you figure out whether the karma will be heavy or light, and why?

- You thought about calling your spouse a derogatory name but didn't speak it out loud.

- You were going to raise your tone at the salesperson for overcharging you but didn't.
- Your significant other yelled at you and you yelled back. You stayed mad for days.
- He went to hit you, so you hit him back.
- You decided to donate your old clothes to charity.
- You gave half your uneaten meal to a person experiencing homelessness as you left a restaurant.
- You go to the soup kitchen and volunteer each week.
- You invited your nephew to stay with you while he was recovering from an accident, nursing him back to health for six months.

What determines how heavy or light the karma will be from actions we take? This depends on many factors.

Intention

Intention, which precedes your thoughts, speech, or actions, is the basis of karma. In general, good intention yields good karma, and vice versa. Consider the following examples:

- You donated $200 to a homeless shelter at the end of the year — so you can benefit from the tax deduction.
- You donated $200 to a homeless shelter at the end of the year — because you know they need help taking care of people when it is cold out.

All things being equal, the second case will generate greater positive karma than the first case. Your motivation was selfless. Intention is the determining factor here.

Object

This refers to the "importance" of the focus of your action of body, speech, or mind. We respect the lives of all sentient beings, from ants to humans. However, harming an ant — all else being equal — will have less of a karmic impact than harming a human being.

Interactions with our parents generate heavier karma, both positive and negative. In fact, our karma connection with our parents is so strong that when the children do something good, it generates good karma for the parents! (and vice versa). Similarly, interactions with our teachers also involve heavier karma.

That is not to say we should treat strangers, insects,

or any other being with less care because the karma is lighter. No! But this knowledge allows us to be aware of the heavier or lighter consequences in the actions we take.

Action

In general, physical actions will have heavier karma than actions of speech. And speaking will have heavier karma than just thinking something (although we can't forget that thoughts are where it all begins). For example, hitting someone will have greater consequence than saying (or thinking) "I'm going to hit you!"

How the action is done also comes into play. Is it done with cruelty? Unintentionally? Is it done with love? Out of compassion for another? Yelling at your child to prevent them from being hit by a car is different from yelling because you lost your temper when they forgot their homework.

Nonetheless actions affect the severity of karmic results.

Completion

How much of the action was completed? Let's consider some examples.

- You offer to help a friend recover from an illness. You say you will prepare his meals for two weeks. You are only able to prepare meals for one week due to a change in your work schedule. Although this action was not completed, there is still good karma associated with what was done.

- You decide to donate $500 to a charity because you know the organization does good work and needs help. After checking your finances, you realize you can only donate $100. Although this action was not completed, here too there is still good karma associated with what was done.

- Similarly, you decide to donate $500 to charity because you know the charity does good work and needs help. After checking your finances, you realize you cannot donate anything. Although this action was not completed, the original intention to donate still has some good karma associated with it, albeit less than in the first two cases.

Becoming Aware of Our Actions

The significance of the karma of any given thought or deed depends on the nature or degree of all four of these factors (intention, object, action, completion).

It is always a good idea to examine real-life examples in order to identify our intention, the object, the action, and the degree of completion. Becoming more aware of our actions, we learn to maximize helping others and minimize harming others (and ourselves).

- How do you speak with your colleagues, friends, and loved ones?
- What are your intentions when you help individuals in your daily life?
- What do you think when you hear, see, or read something you don't approve of?

The more we know about ourselves, the easier it is to improve and reduce the actions that create negative karma.

Distorted View

An individual may act based on a misunderstanding of the situation. For example, you think your significant other is cheating on you, but they are not. Because of your misunderstanding, you take drastic, harmful action. You may think you are 100 percent justified, but you are not. When you act based on a distorted view of a situation, karma is heavier.

Lack of Antidote or Regret

In chapter 8, we will learn how to implement antidotes that will purify our negative karma. One aspect of purification involves developing a feeling of regret for what you did.

When an individual takes an action and continues to justify it in their own mind instead of feeling regret, the karma is heavier. The beauty of the antidotes we can practice is they not only reduce the severity of the karma but also motivate us to reduce our chances of repeating the act.

Subject

If the person doing the action is a child, ignorant, or mentally disabled, then the karma will not be as heavy either. As children grow, they become more and more responsible for their actions, as in any legal system. The same is true regarding karma.

EXERCISE

Think of something you did today and identify the intention that preceded it, the object of your action, the type of action you took, and the degree of completion. Do you think the karma was heavy, light, or somewhere in between? Why?

CHAPTER 3

Where Is Karma Stored?

Karma is like a memory stored in our conscious-ness. Our mind is the ground and home of karma.

According to Western science, memory is stored in various regions of our brain and nervous system. When talking about the seeds of karma, we are refer-ring to the traces and impressions that are left on our consciousness.

Our mind stream is the continuous sequence of our mental activity, awareness, and the moment-to-moment flow of what our senses and mind experience. Many Buddhists believe that the impressions that make up our mind stream are not only from this lifetime, but also from all past lifetimes.

The karmic seeds are stored in our consciousness until they ripen. And when they do, we experience the results of our karma. In other words, these seeds have the potential to bring about the result of our karmic actions. This will be explored further in chapter 4.

And as we will see in chapter 5, our mind becomes conditioned when we take certain actions repeatedly. Our neural pathways become strengthened as we allow habits to develop, making them harder to break.

Using the agriculture metaphor again, the field where we plant crops is analogous to our field of consciousness. As we think, speak, and act, we plant seeds in our mind. Our mind "records" these actions just like a memory. And just like planting vegetables or flowers, not all seeds sprout at the same time. Some sprout more quickly than others due to the many variables that impact growth (e.g., rain, sun, fertilizer, wind, size of the seeds).

As we saw in chapter 1, many attributes describe karma. And as we saw in chapter 2, many factors determine the strength of karma, such as intention, object, action, and completion. Given these factors and attributes, which in many cases are not easily measured, the complexity and sophistication of karma should be apparent.

To continue the analogy, we may have a field where we plant seeds for apple trees, roses, tomatoes, corn, carrots, weeds, and so much more. Each seed will mature and sprout subject to the variables mentioned above. The consequences of our karmic actions sprout and mature at different times, also subject to numerous variables. And since they are all stored in the same field of consciousness, they can affect one another as well.

EXERCISE

Identify one food at your next meal and review the number of people and actions involved in getting it to your table.

CHAPTER 4

When Do We Experience the Results of Our Karma?

When does our karma come to fruition?

- If you punch someone in the face, your karma can come back almost immediately — with a punch to your own face.
- If you break the law in a very visible way, your karma can come back quickly as well.
- If you volunteer at a soup kitchen, the karmic reward may start to manifest the moment you help someone who shows incredible gratitude. And in the future, when you are in need, others may step up to help you in turn.

Now is a good time to address the question we all ask: Why do some "bad" people seem to have good things happen to them, while "good" people have bad things happen to them? Where is the karma in those situations?

In some cases, it may be easy to see that actions taken today may produce results far in the future. Financial investing is a good example of just that. We invest money now to receive financial benefits in the future. We may not see those benefits right away, or at all. The process takes time, and there are many risk factors at play.

Likewise, karmic seeds planted in your mind can ripen immediately or in the future. The future includes both this lifetime and lifetimes to come.

Once again, let's use the analogy of planting vegetable seeds in a field. When do they ripen? And how good will they taste? That depends on many variables: sun, earth, fertilizer, water, how much sun, how much water, when were they watered, the size of the seeds, the quantity of seeds, the condition of the ground, the season they were planted, et cetera.

How often do we read about someone who committed a crime and was found not guilty due to a technicality? Or their attorneys were able to find a way to get them off? One might ask, "Where is the karma? Where is the justice?"

You can be assured that the results of their karma await them. The justice system's role in meting out karmic consequences is much narrower than the broader law of karma. Regardless of whether individuals who commit crimes pay a price legally, they may spend the rest of their lives in their own hell, wishing they had acted differently or always looking over their shoulder out of fear of being caught.

Of course, there are many people who do "bad" things and have no regrets whatsoever. Their karma will come to fruition — if not in this lifetime, then certainly in lifetimes to come.

And finally, most of us cannot truly "see" someone's karma, even our own. Although there are some great masters who have that capability, it is not something we can or need to do. As spiritual seekers, our job is to do the best we can starting now and moving forward. Karma will take care of the rest.

EXERCISE

Think of something that happened to you today that was the result of an action you took a long time ago.

CHAPTER 5

Karma and Habits Are Synonyms?

A nother way to look at karma is that it is a type of habit, but not of the "brush your teeth daily" or "be on time" variety. The habits we are referring to are the ways we view ourselves and our identity, which are created and perpetuated by all the stories we tell ourselves. These repetitive stories are habits that solidify our sense of identity.

These stories are your personal movie about who you are. You may tell yourself that you are a good parent or employee, or that you are generous, smart, and pretty. This PR film starring you is very long.

You have stories running through your mind about different fears in both real and imagined circumstances. There are hundreds of ways to describe how you view yourself. And those stories and beliefs change from day to day or even moment to moment.

Lastly, such beliefs don't even have to be true. As the Dude says in the 1998 cult film *The Big Lebowski*, "Yeah, well, you know, that's just, like, your opinion, man."

Let's consider two examples:

- It is your belief you are generous. You give five dollars today to a person experiencing homelessness. You feel good because you know most people don't give anything. After sharing your story of generosity with a friend, he calls you a cheapskate. He says, "You should have given him twenty dollars. You can't even buy a good meal for five dollars anymore." You tell your son, and he can't believe you wasted your money like that. You start to rethink whether you are generous.

- You think you are an "on time" person. You arrive at work every day at 9:00 a.m., if not sooner. You always head to the airport early. When you meet friends, you get there before anyone else arrives. One evening, at 6:00 p.m., you are in the car waiting for your husband so you can meet friends for dinner. As usual, your husband is running late. It is now 6:07 and he is just walking out the front door. You will be late to your dinner date. The next day you arrive at work at 9:04 a.m. You don't think much of it, because it's only four minutes. And you know that no one noticed. So are you an "on time" person or not? Clearly the answer can change from day to day, even moment to moment.

These views of ourselves are always a moving target. They are beliefs, judgments, or opinions — not facts. And because they are not facts, but rather a repetitive set or pattern of changing views and opinions, they are inconsistent and illusory. They are certainly not stable or accurate. But the more you replay, reinforce, and solidify them, the more solid and "factual" you make them in your mind.

When you encounter a situation or another person's view that conflicts with your view of yourself, you may become triggered. You may experience discomfort, irritation, anger, confusion, anxiety, or fear.

- You think you are on time, but your significant other says, "No! You are late half the time."
- You think you are a good employee, but your boss gives you a less than stellar review.

- You think you are a good businessperson, but a pandemic puts your company out of business.
- You think you do a good job caring for your lawn, but your neighbor is critical of the few weeds that remain.

We see this a lot in the professional world. Our careers play a large part in how we view ourselves. You think you are a caring, skillful physician. But once in a blue moon a patient complains because you may have been too direct (for their taste) or you didn't spend enough time with them (from their perspective). This hits you at the heart of your self-identity. But everyone has a different opinion of who you are as a healthcare practitioner, which can change from day to day as well.

This is not a matter of truth. It's a matter of someone having a different perspective from the view you have of yourself. These views are just strong opinions about ourselves and the world, but we hold on to them as facts. The habits we are talking about are these opinions, preferences, views, and stories that run through our minds.

The way we see ourselves is a type of karmic action too. Actions, speech, and thoughts that reinforce our self-identity create negative karma. Actions that loosen our self-identity create positive karma.

In Buddhism, trying to hold on to something illusory is an example of "mistaken view." We think our identity is solid, when it is just a lot of thoughts we have repeated to ourselves until we accept them as facts.

The more certain of who we think we are, the more we are trying to hold on to something illusory and inconsistent. This creates negative karma. We create positive karma when we think of others first.

So how do you know what your habits are, or how strong they are? It's actually quite simple.

The next time you notice you are angry, irritated, anxious, or fearful, stop and examine the situation. What triggered this state of mind? Someone or something is conflicting with your strong view of yourself. And that grasping of a view of yourself is a habit.

You know how self-centered you are by how often you experience negative states of mind and how intense your reaction and response are to any conflicting view. These negative states of mind reflect your resistance to another perspective, as you try to defend your "self" against the opposing views.

We are not talking about truth here. We are talking

about our strong opinion of ourselves as being something permanent. This misunderstanding is the definition of "ignorance" in Buddhism.

How much we grasp and cling are habits — or karma — embedded in our consciousness. That karma follows us through our lifetime and into the next, unless we purify, transfer, or dilute it.

Another way to look at it is that holding on to illusions harms us during our lifetime. We are prisoners to our own thoughts. And our karma/habits/illusions determine the state of mind we have as we die. That same level of grasping at the self continues through the afterlife and is what is reborn in a new body, unless we start now to reduce it.

By diminishing our self-centered nature, we create positive karma and experience a greater sense of liberation — now.

Shantideva, the eighth-century Buddhist monk, poet, and scholar, states it beautifully:

> All those who are unhappy in the world are so as a
>   result of their desire for their own happiness.
> All those who are happy in the world are so as
>   a result of their desire for the happiness of
>   others.

EXERCISE

What habit (i.e., strong self-centered view) do you see in yourself that you would like to break? Review your day and identify a desire of how you wish something in your life should be different. This could be anything, from wanting more money or sex to desiring more intimacy or a better job. Identify how many times a day you think about it.

CHAPTER 6

How Do You Start Creating
Positive Karma?

It is hard to fix something if you don't know it's broken. So the first thing we need to do is train ourselves to be aware of our thoughts. Once again, karma starts with the mind, and specifically with our intention. As Lama Lhanang puts it:

> Our mind is the king of our karma.
> Our speech and thoughts are the ministers of the karma.
> Our hands and legs are the soldiers of the karma.
> Time is the weapon of the soldiers.
> But it is not up to the soldiers or the ministers.
> It is up to the king.
> Our mind is the real decision-maker.

Mind

By training ourselves to be mindful of the motivation behind our actions, speech, and thoughts, we can decide the best way to respond to any situation we encounter. In the Dhammapada, an ancient collection of teachings attributed to the Buddha, it is said:

> Mind precedes all mental states. Mind is their chief; they are all mind-wrought. If with an impure mind a person speaks or acts, suffering follows him like the wheel that follows the foot of the ox.
>
> Mind precedes all mental states. Mind is their chief; they are all mind-wrought. If with a pure mind a person speaks or acts, happiness follows him like his never-departing shadow.

If thoughts precede actions of speech and body, then examining our thoughts is the best way to get to the root of karma. Through simple and consistent meditation practice, we can develop the ability to observe and identify what we are thinking about.

Meditating is easy to do! Anyone who tells you differently has not been taught well or has incorrect expectations, either of which is a formula for frustration and failure. Meditation may be hard to do *well*, but its benefits are still achieved through consistent practice.

The merits can be described in so many ways. For the sake of brevity, here are just a few of the benefits of sitting meditation:

- learning how to deal calmly with chaos around you
- learning how to manage stress
- experiencing peace of mind
- developing clarity of mind
- cultivating sensitivity toward yourself and others
- knowing who you are
- improving physical health
- gaining a sense of liberation from negative states of mind

How badly you want those rewards will determine whether and how consistently you meditate. Here are a few cues to motivate your practice:

- Your state of mind is the only thing you can control, and meditation is the first step toward doing so.

- How your mind works determines your degree of freedom, joy, and happiness.
- The key to observing your mind is meditation.

There are countless ways to meditate. Sometimes the simplest is the best, which is why in appendix A we describe a highly effective meditation on observing your breath.

Another way to view how negative karma starts in the mind is by examining our mental states. Buddhists have identified the seeds of our negative karma as the Five Poisons. If you rid yourself of any of these poisons, you are free from karma! They are ignorance, attachment, aversion, pride, and envy.

1. Ignorance describes not seeing or understanding the way things are (e.g., seeing our self as stable and solid, viewing the world around us as permanent).
2. Attachment refers to how we can grasp on to desires or preferences (e.g., desire for money, power, sex).
3. Aversion refers to all the people, places, and things we don't like and therefore resist or push away.

4. Pride is when we have an inflated opinion of ourselves, especially when compared to others.

5. Envy is when we are jealous of others.

With meditation we can start to consider the following questions:

- Can you identify when you observe these disturbances in your mind?
- Do you notice repetitive thoughts passing through your mind?
- Do you notice negative thoughts about people, places, and things?
- Do you notice the strong opinions and preferences you have? Do they get stronger every time a particular situation arises?
- Do you notice how your thoughts affect your state of mind and how you feel?
- Do you notice how many of your thoughts are about the past (which cannot be changed) or the future (which is unknown)?

You have already begun to rewire your brain.

You would never walk into a bad neighborhood at night. The same is true about where your mind spends its time. You can avoid spending time with negative thoughts, grasping desires, or wishes that repeat over and over.

When you notice these thoughts, you can "change the channel" and think about something else! You can let the thoughts pass through without grasping on to them, depriving them of their power. When triggered, you can practice repeating a mantra, saying a prayer, or just refocusing your attention on your breath. These tools are wonderful ways to bring your mind back to the present, rather than dwelling on the past or worrying about the future. As Lama Lhanang says, "The past is history, the future is mystery, the present moment is a gift."

Now you can start to examine how many of your thoughts or opinions are actually true. As time passes, you may gain perspective on something you were sure of, only to realize you were mistaken. Not everything you think is true! We can see that holding tight to our opinions (thinking they are facts) is what causes our negative states of mind. As the old saying goes, "It ain't what you don't know that gets you in trouble, it's what you know for sure that just ain't so."

You don't have to believe everything you think!

You can start to examine your intention prior to acting, speaking, and thinking. Are you motivated by self-interest or care for others? In essence, your karma is always positive if your primary motivation is to benefit someone else.

Actions

Now that we know that our mind (i.e., thoughts) precedes our physical actions, let's look at the actions of our body. What actions create good karma? What actions create negative karma? The Buddha went into detail on this topic in a teaching to his son Rahula:

> "What do you think, Rahula: What is a mirror for?"
>
> "For reflection, sir."
>
> "In the same way, Rahula, bodily actions, verbal actions, & mental actions are to be done with repeated reflection.
>
> "Whenever you want to do a bodily action, you should reflect on it: 'This bodily action I want to do — would it lead to self-affliction, to the affliction of others, or to both? Would it be an unskillful bodily action, with

painful consequences, painful results?' If, on reflection, you know that it would lead to self-affliction, to the affliction of others, or to both; it would be an unskillful bodily action with painful consequences, painful results, then any bodily action of that sort is absolutely unfit for you to do. But if on reflection you know that it would not cause affliction…it would be a skillful bodily action with pleasant consequences, pleasant results, then any bodily action of that sort is fit for you to do."

The Buddha goes on to emphasize reflecting on actions not only beforehand, but also during and after. While doing an action, "If, on reflection, you know that it is leading to self-affliction, to the affliction of others, or to both…you should give it up. But if on reflection you know that it is not…you may continue with it." After doing an action:

If, on reflection, you know that it led to self-affliction, to the affliction of others, or to both; it was an unskillful bodily action with painful consequences, painful results, then you should confess it, reveal it, lay it open to the Teacher or to a knowledgeable companion in the holy life. Having confessed it…you should exercise restraint in the future. But if on reflection you know that it did not lead to affliction…it was a skillful bodily action with pleasant consequences, pleasant results, then you should stay mentally refreshed & joyful, training day & night in skillful mental qualities.

The Buddha taught this succinctly in this short quote: "He who harms living beings is, for that reason, not an ariya (a Noble One); he who does not harm any living being is called an ariya." What actions cause harm and which do not? We see that this teaching leaves much to the individual's judgment, as it should. Based on the guidelines, you decide whether your intention involves harming or benefiting living beings. (Refer back to chapter 2 for evaluating the karma of your actions.)

The Buddha taught that we should not harm living beings, which includes all sentient beings, not just humans. In this regard, from an ethical perspective, there are many excellent reasons for being a vegetarian or a vegan. From a health perspective, there are many reasons to eat meat, poultry, or fish in moderation. Many practitioners are vegetarians or vegans, which is wonderful. Many others still enjoy eating meat or fish for health or culinary reasons, and that is their choice.

Here is an accommodation that we have found to be very successful. If you or your family eats meat or fish five times a week, consider cutting it down to four. If you or your family eats meat or fish four times a week, consider cutting it down to three. *Any* reduction in eating meat or fish will save many animals from suffering.

As with any diet, preparation is key. This includes getting agreement from your family or household members, preparing food, and planning alternative meals. All of this is voluntary. No one is keeping track. It is between you and your family.

And for those who do eat meat or fish, we suggest reciting the Four Immeasurables prior to meals:

May all beings have happiness and the cause of
　happiness.
May they be free of suffering and the cause of
　suffering.
May they never be separated from the great
　happiness which is without suffering.

> May they abide in the boundless equanimity, free
> from attachment and aversion.

You may have a prayer that is more meaningful to you or to your beliefs. That is OK! Reciting this prayer will make us conscious of the life that was taken for our enjoyment and nutrition, allowing us to appreciate what we have. And most important, it will have an impact on the consciousness of the animal that died for your meal so that it may be reborn in a better situation.

The Buddha's main point is simple and clear. Do no harm.

Speech

Right speech is one of the Eightfold Path teachings that the Buddha preached immediately after becoming enlightened. How can speech do any harm? It's just words coming out of someone's mouth! You would think it's not that big a deal. And nevertheless, it is one of the most important karmic actions we can do, for good or bad. Lama Lhanang's view is that "one word can change somebody's life. One word can destroy somebody's life."

Right speech is so important that the Buddha

taught it many times throughout his life, such as when he said, "It is spoken at the right time. It is spoken in truth. It is spoken affectionately. It is spoken beneficially. It is spoken with a mind of good-will." On another occasion, the Buddha instructed King Abhaya on the topic:

> In the case of words that the [Buddha] knows
>   to be unfactual, untrue, unbeneficial,
>   unendearing & disagreeable to others, he does
>   not say them.

> In the case of words that the [Buddha] knows to
>   be factual, true, unbeneficial, unendearing &
>   disagreeable to others, he does not say them.

> In the case of words that the [Buddha] knows to
>   be factual, true, beneficial, but unendearing
>   & disagreeable to others, he has a sense of the
>   proper time for saying them.

> In the case of words that the [Buddha] knows
>   to be unfactual, untrue, unbeneficial, but
>   endearing & agreeable to others, he does not
>   say them.

In the case of words that the [Buddha] knows to
be factual, true, unbeneficial, but endearing &
agreeable to others, he does not say them.

In the case of words that the [Buddha] knows
to be factual, true, beneficial, and endearing
& agreeable to others, he has a sense of the
proper time for saying them. Why is that?
Because the [Buddha] has sympathy for living
beings.

Shantideva is similarly clear on when to speak and
what to do if speaking is not appropriate. And although
the following advice may seem simplistic, its results are
powerful, practical, and effective:

When one intends to move or when one intends to
speak, one should first examine one's own mind
and then act appropriately with composure.

When one sees one's mind to be attached or
repulsed, then one should neither act nor
speak, but remain still like a piece of wood.

When my mind is haughty, sarcastic, full of
conceit and arrogance, ridiculing, evasive and

deceitful, when it is inclined to boast, or when
it is contemptuous of others, abusive, and
irritable, then I should remain still like a piece
of wood.

When my mind seeks material gain, honor, and
fame, or when it seeks attendants and service,
then I will remain still like a piece of wood.

When my mind is averse to the interests of
others and seeks my own self-interest, or
when it wishes to speak out of a desire for an
audience, then I will remain still like a piece
of wood.

When it is impatient, indolent, timid, impudent,
garrulous, or biased in my own favor, then I
will remain still like a piece of wood.

In summary, we now see that all karma starts with
our mind and its thoughts. We can learn about our
mind through study, contemplation, and meditation.
This knowledge of ourselves and our perspective gives
us a more accurate view of ourselves and those around
us. It is a wonderful start as we travel the path to im-
proved mental health and liberation from suffering. As

we modify our actions of mind, body, and speech, over time we reap the benefits of good karma.

Buddhists have compiled a list of ten nonvirtuous actions that, when enacted, create negative karma. Abstaining from any of these behaviors is a virtuous act and creates positive karma! And no worries, there is a complementary list of ten virtuous actions that are even more effective for positive karma. See appendix B for these invaluable resources.

EXERCISE

What action of body, speech, or mind today would you do differently if the same situation comes up tomorrow?

CHAPTER 7

So Just Create Positive Karma
and Reduce Negative Karma?

In short, yes! To be free of negative states of mind, we must eliminate our bad habits and self-centered predilections. As mentioned above, we will then be able to live calmly, peacefully, and joyfully, even amid chaos.

It is a noble pursuit and a lifelong effort. Breaking the habit of the Five Poisons takes time and perseverance. For many it may require a whole lifetime or even many lifetimes to achieve.

Great practitioners of all religions are free from the Five Poisons described in chapter 6. Their minds are pure. Through years of study, contemplation, meditation, and introspection, they become liberated. In fact, great beings no longer create karma.

- They have no grasping.
- They have no self-centered habits or desires.

- They have no fear.
- They have no identity to protect.
- They are just inhabiting their bodies until it is time to go.
- They are selfless, kind, generous, and wise.

Their concern is no longer for themselves but only for the well-being of others. We have many role models in this pursuit: Jesus, Mother Teresa, Moses, Buddha, His Holiness the Fourteenth Dalai Lama, Archbishop Desmond Tutu, and Thich Nhat Hanh, to name a few.

We can even look closer to home to our friends and neighbors who help us when we are in need. We see the brave valor of our healthcare workers who risk their lives to help those suffering during the Covid pandemic. At such times these individuals are truly selfless.

Great beings feel the suffering of the world's inhabitants so deeply that their only concern is to reduce the suffering of all sentient beings. Through years of practice, by their selflessness, they transcend karma. They are no longer triggered by what goes on around them. They do not repeat self-centered habits. Their only wish is to help others.

And when such figures are ill, many show no change in their kind, generous, even upbeat persona. As we all know, most people when ill suffer physically and mentally. Not so with great beings. They can control their state of mind to avoid entertaining negative thoughts. It is a wonderful teaching to be able to see this happen. In Tibetan Buddhism, great masters accept that experiencing illness is paying off their karmic debt from less skillful actions in their past.

EXERCISE

Before going to sleep, review your day. See if you can identify any actions (of body, speech, and mind) that were in retrospect selfish or selfless. Were you able to dilute any of your negative karma with positive karma today? Were there any actions you could have done better?

CHAPTER 8

How Do You Reduce the Negative Karma You Created Earlier in Life?

From a Tibetan Buddhist perspective, we can change or even eliminate our karma in several ways. Changing your karma requires that you start from the bottom of your heart. These are not mechanistic behaviors that can be changed by flipping a switch.

We must first recognize that we are not free from karma. Before doing our best to reduce or eliminate our impurities, we must understand how karma works. Simply put, if you want to change your karma you need to study it first.

With that in mind, here are three powerful, tried-and-true methods that can reduce or eliminate our negative karma and increase our positive karma.

Dilution

As we create more positive karma and less negative karma, we dilute any negative karma we have already created. Let's say you spend your whole life speaking poorly of others, blaming them for whatever triggers you, deceiving yourself and others, being angry or selfish. Then you become aware of it. You start to act selflessly and alter your behavior. By doing so, the equation changes. You are diluting your negative karma by creating positive karma going forward.

The negative karma doesn't go away from dilution, but its effects are mitigated. Negative karma from our past is like a big lump of salt. If you put it in a glass with just a bit of water, it is way too salty to drink. But if you put it into a large body of water, like a river, the water becomes drinkable.

The river symbolizes a virtuous and unselfish mind. We reduce our negative karma by doing more positive actions and fewer negative actions.

Once again, there is no better time to start then now!

Purification

We can purify our negative karma. Purification practices are an important focus of chanting and prayers in Tibetan schools of Buddhism. These are best taught in person by a qualified Buddhist teacher. For purification practices to be effective, practitioners must be dedicated and committed to performing them intensively and correctly. The more you dedicate yourself to this practice, the more it will work for you.

Purification includes the following steps:

1. Meditation, where we connect with a higher being or presence (from any religion).
2. Admission or confession (to that higher presence) of the actions that created the negative karma.
3. Remorse for one's actions.
4. Resolution not to repeat the actions that caused the negative karma.
5. Commitment to creating positive karma.
6. Dedication of that positive karma to beings who are suffering.

These actions work to rid us of the habits that created negative karma. And we learn in the process to develop more selfless behavior going forward. The practice is liberating, cleansing, and effective.

Transference

At the time of death, we can release ourselves of our negative karma and transfer our consciousness to a higher being. Once again, these practices are best taught in person by a qualified Buddhist teacher. Likewise, for transference practices to be effective, the practitioner must be dedicated and committed to practicing them intensively and correctly. The amount of dedication you put into this practice is directly proportional to how much it will work for you.

Regardless of what you have done in the past, according to the great lamas, dedicated practice is the quickest way to reach enlightenment. Motivation is the basis of success in this practice.

Many Tibetan Buddhist practitioners practice Phowa (which means "release"), a combination of visualization, yoga, and mantra. It is primarily associated with visualizing ourselves as a being free from all karma and then merging our consciousness with a higher being at the end of life. Performing Phowa while dying reduces or eliminates the burden of negative karma that the practitioner has accumulated.

There is an abbreviated version of Phowa included

in appendix C. It may be read softly and slowly to the dying person. When reciting, it is best to sit close to their head so that the softness of your voice can merge into their being.

It can be practiced by the living as well. Many Tibetan Buddhists perform Phowa on a regular basis. Familiarizing the practitioner with the prospect of death helps to reduce their negative karma.

It is helpful for anyone in the dying phase of life to "lighten" the burden they may feel. We are surrendering ourselves to a higher being. And by doing so, we are relieved. Our negative karma is released.

After all, the simple act of surrendering to a higher being is a selfless act, which by definition creates positive karma. After several recitations, the practitioner will be able to perform Phowa on their own. The more they practice, the greater the love they will feel as they pass on.

Also included in appendix C is another reading, titled "Encouragement." This can help our loved ones be at ease with letting go of the past and moving forward without stress or regret. Once again, it is best to sit close to their head so you can read to them softly and with love.

EXERCISE

Identify one action (of body, speech, or mind) that you did today that you know may have been self-centered and possibly at the expense of someone else.

- Take a few minutes to observe your breath as your mind calms.
- Identify with any higher being or presence you find inspiring. This can be from any religion.
- Confess to that higher presence the actions that created the negative karma.
- Express regret to yourself and the higher being.
- Express determination that you will do your best to not repeat that action.
- Commit to continue helping sentient beings, and when you do, dedicating the fruits of that effort to those who are suffering.

CHAPTER 9

What Happens to Your Karma When You Die?

Our karma (habits), which are stored in our field of consciousness, continue through the afterlife. The bardo (as it's known in Tibetan) is the gap between the time of our death in this body and our rebirth in another body. It is like a dream state, but without the physical body sleeping in bed, of course.

Our dream state while we are alive reflects our mind. If we go to sleep angry, our dreams will reflect that. So too our consciousness's experience in the bardo reflects our karma. Our body and brain are dead and gone. The only thing that continues is the karmic traces stored in our consciousness.

If our strong habits include anger, jealousy, or attachment to self in myriad ways, then our consciousness will contain those karmic traces. Our bardo experience, as well as our rebirth, will reflect those habits. Wherever you go there you are.

And since our karma continues to our next life-time, it determines how, where, in what family, in what country, and in what condition we are reborn. Our current way of living — that is, the degree of our grasping and clinging to the illusion of self — determines not just the next moment, next minute, next day, or next week, but our experience in the afterlife and whether we have an auspicious rebirth.

Here are common situations where we create karma by grasping and telling ourselves stories to support our identity. The amount we judge ourselves or cling to our perspective determines whether the karma we create is negative or positive.

- "I get anxious when my bank account gets too low." This can be an attachment to our view of ourselves as being financially successful. What will people think if I can't afford my expenses and must move to a smaller home?
- "I want people to like me." This can be an attachment to how we view ourselves as likable, better, good, sharp, cool, or smart. We fear that

others might think of us differently than we think of ourselves.

- "I am afraid of failing." This can be an attachment to how we view ourselves as successful, normal, or good at something. The way we think of ourselves might be different than the way others think of us.

- "I argue with my wife all the time." This can be an attachment to the need to be right. This supports our sense of self. If she is right, then my self-view must be wrong.

- "I am afraid of being intimate. I fear being rejected." This can be an attachment to our self, in that someone else might view me differently from how I view myself.

Whenever someone or some situation shows me that my self-image is not what I've been holding on to all my life, I feel resistance, fear, and anxiety. These feelings indicate that I have developed these types of habits.

How we deal with these situations creates impressions in our consciousness. Eliminating fears and self-cherishing actions and reactions creates positive karma; failing to do so creates negative karma. Just as in the 1993 film *Groundhog Day*, situations we face in this lifetime will continue to arise until we are able to deal with them skillfully.

As stated in chapter 5, our aim is to reduce our attachment to ourselves by being more open-minded about our identity and avoiding the reinforcement of illusory beliefs. Karma is the aspect of our consciousness that persists after we die. In our next life, our consciousness is reborn in the womb of our mother as another sentient being.

EXERCISE

Identify a view you have about who you think you are. Consider that this perception may not be accurate. Can you allow for a more flexible view of yourself?

CHAPTER 10

What If I Don't Believe in Rebirth?

Not everyone believes in rebirth, reincarnation, or future lives. The concept of karma — encapsulated by the common phrase "what goes around comes around" — is universally relatable. Taking that saying to heart can motivate us to effectively reduce our negative karma and improve our lives and the lives of those around us in this lifetime.

We can all agree that our actions today will affect others during this lifetime and even after we are gone. To see our impact on those we leave behind, let's consider a broader understanding of rebirth.

Thich Nhat Hanh was a Vietnamese Zen Buddhist monk, peace activist, prolific author, poet, teacher, and founder of the Plum Village Tradition. He is known as the "father of mindfulness." His poem "Oneness" begins with a beautiful description of rebirth:

The moment I die,
I will try to come back to you
as quickly as possible.
I promise it will not take long.

Kansas poet Clare Harner wrote the now famous death poem "Immortality," which captures the ephemeral and everlasting nature after death as well.

Do not stand
　　By my grave, and weep.
I am not there,
　　I do not sleep —
I am the thousand winds that blow
I am the diamond glints in snow
I am the sunlight on ripened grain,
I am the gentle, autumn rain.
As you awake with morning's hush,
I am the swift, up-flinging rush
Of quiet birds in circling flight,
I am the day transcending night.
Do not stand
　　By my grave, and cry —
I am not there,
　　I did not die.

EXERCISE

Imagine that you have died.

- What impact will your life have had on those who live on?
- Consider the memories that will live on with colleagues, friends, and family.
- Consider the broader impact that your life had on people you never met.

CHAPTER 11

What Does Collective Karma Mean?

In chapter 1, we discussed that karma is the way our personal ethical world operates. The concept of collective karma also exists.

Madame Blavatsky of the Theosophical Society first suggested this term in the early 1900s. It refers to a situation in which a group of people experience harm or death, such as a natural disaster or a war. Sometimes it is used to suggest that the group who was harmed or killed is somehow responsible for their own injury or demise.

This non-Buddhist concept is not accurate. It is easy to blame people for what happens to them. We have seen responsibility unfairly placed on many groups of suffering beings:

- the six million Jews who perished in the Holocaust.

- the 230,000 people who died during the Indian Ocean tsunami in 2014.
- the West Africans who were brought to America as slaves between the sixteenth and nineteenth centuries.

Let's examine the group of people who decided to harm another group. A group is a collection of individuals. And each person that is part of a "group" decision to harm others has their own individual karma. As we have discussed, each person who decided to take those harmful actions will reap negative karma.

There is no "collective action" that creates "collective karma." It only appears that way in these extreme cases. For example, a country and its population go to war. But the decision to go to war was made by individuals in government positions, who were supported by those who elected them to office and those who carried out the killing.

We can determine individual responsibility if there is a direct connection between action and consequence in this lifetime. Hitler and his followers made decisions that created the calamity that was the Third Reich. At the time, many Germans supported his despicable actions. Those individuals who have gone to war and committed atrocities will face the consequences either in this lifetime or in future lifetimes.

Now let's consider the people who were harmed or killed by war. From a Buddhist perspective, the events of World War II lie squarely on the shoulders of those who caused them *in this lifetime*.

However, we do not hold people responsible for actions they took in previous lifetimes. It is impossible to determine the cause and effect of multiple lives. We only hold people responsible for their actions in their current incarnation.

Blame or fault is never the focus when we look at karmic actions that may have taken place many lifetimes ago. The Buddhist focus is on acting now to prevent it from happening again. We are individuals and we all must learn from our mistakes.

EXERCISE

Consider the decisions made by those who committed genocide versus those made by the people who chose to help the victims. In both cases their karma placed them at that moment in time. While some chose to perpetuate the horrific acts, others chose not to. In what situations do you find yourself where you have the choice to perpetuate your negative karma or change it?

CHAPTER 12

What's Karma Got to Do with It?

W ho doesn't want to be liberated from all the suffering we experience? We all want freedom. But let's be clear on what this means. It doesn't mean being happy all the time. It doesn't mean everything will go our way. It doesn't mean everyone will agree with us. If the world always cooperated with our moment's desires, we wouldn't need this book!

As Lama Lhanang reminds his students, "When the weather is sunny and the food is good, anyone can be a good [Buddhist] practitioner." Liberation means we are free from our habits of clinging to who we think we are. It means we decide how we respond when a potential trigger arises. We are no longer subject to the old responses we have been using our entire lives. They no longer serve us.

Liberation means learning to control ourselves so

that when things go wrong, we don't lose our minds. It means pausing before we react and thereby responding skillfully. It means understanding we are responsible for our own freedom.

Here is Shantideva's case for taking charge of our own state of mind:

> Where would there be leather enough to cover the entire world?
> The earth is covered over merely with the leather of my sandals.

We can break the habit of reacting negatively to what happens around us. We have both the conceptual understanding and the practical tools to change. We now know we are responsible for how we navigate our lives. We can do it with either love and compassion or anger and jealousy. We can choose to be triggered by what happens around us — or not. We can allow ourselves to create habits that will continually harm us and others — or not. We can become the drivers of our own life by breaking the habits of grasping, clinging, and propping up our illusory self-identity.

As mentioned above, Lama Lhanang teaches, "The

past is history. The future is a mystery. The present moment is a gift." The present moment is a gift. Why? Because at any time, we can bring our attention to it. We can observe our breathing whenever we want. We can use this tool to break the habit of the stories that run through our mind, especially when we are triggered. Not only can we come back to the present moment, we can even train ourselves to stay there more and more.

We can't change the past. We have no idea what the future brings. But we can live in the present moment. We can reduce or eliminate our negative karma, which stems from our tendency to hold on to illusory thoughts or opinions. Let's reverse the habits we have developed. Our backstory is irrelevant, as is how we arrived here.

Freedom and liberation are available. As Lama Lhanang reminds us, it's up to you:

> The Buddha can't wash away your karma.
> He can't take it away.
> You created your karma.
> You have to work on it yourself.

EXERCISE

Can you think of one storyline in the next hour? As soon as you do, observe your breath for three to five seconds.

APPENDIX A

An Easy Meditation for You

Y ou can do this anywhere, anytime. No additional tools are required.

- Take ten minutes to sit peacefully with your eyes closed.
- Observe your breath as you inhale and exhale.
- Breathe naturally, without trying to change anything.
- Watch your breath in its natural state as it passes through your nostrils.
- Observe the inhale, observe the exhale, and observe any pause in between.
- Sometimes your breathing is shallow, sometimes it is deep. No matter — just notice without any modification whatsoever.
- If you find yourself distracted by your thoughts

or sounds, don't worry. Just return to observing your breath.

It is as simple with that. Start by doing this once a day. After a while, if you feel inclined, you can practice twice a day!

Set yourself up for success. Choose a comfortable chair or cushion to sit on. Create an environment for meditation with minimal distractions. Keep it clean. Hang inspiring images or quotes in your meditation area. Simplicity is key. Furnish the room so that it feels special.

Mornings are a good time for meditation — before you eat, before you start your day, before your mind is off to the races. Evenings work as well, but not after a full meal and not when you are too tired to stay awake.

At the beginning of your session, the mind might be resistant and filled with thoughts. This is not a problem — just go back to observing your breath. Treat it like playing a game. Enjoy the process.

Make no judgments before, during, or after. The benefits are there, regardless of how well you think you are doing.

After practicing consistently, preferably daily for a few weeks, you will notice the parade of thoughts that pop up during the day. You are becoming more aware of your mind and how it spends its time.

Ten Nonvirtuous and
Ten Virtuous Actions

Nonvirtuous: Killing is when you take the life of any sentient being.

Virtuous: Support animal life. Have compassion for all living beings.

Nonvirtuous: Stealing refers to taking something without permission, through means such as theft, cheating, or deception.

Virtuous: Be generous.

Nonvirtuous: Sexual misconduct refers to sexual activity that is nonconsensual, disrespectful, or abusive.

Virtuous: Be kind with your sexual activity.

Nonvirtuous: Lying can be categorized as outright lies, white lies, or even just giving a wrong impression.

Virtuous: Be honest, authentic, and compassionate with your right speech.

Nonvirtuous: Divisive talk is speech that divides people. This can be achieved through explicit or subtle nuances in how you communicate.

Virtuous: Be inclusive. Even when surrounded by those with differing opinions, be skillful with your speech.

Nonvirtuous: Harsh speech refers to speech where the intention is to harm someone.

Virtuous: Find something positive to say.

Nonvirtuous: Idle talk refers to complaining, gossiping, or criticism that is meant to harm, and includes speaking poorly of another individual.

Virtuous: Silence can be golden, even sacred.

Nonvirtuous: Craving is when you desire something someone else has. This includes material things as well as qualities, such as health, intelligence, and appearance.

Virtuous: Be grateful for what you have.

Nonvirtuous: Ill will is the act of wishing bad things on another person or being happy when another person suffers a loss.

Virtuous: Rejoice in the well-being of others.

Nonvirtuous: Wrong view is when you do not understand the cause-and-effect nature of life, thinking you can "get away" with unwholesome behavior.

Virtuous: Research the results of your actions of body, speech, and mind. You be the judge.

The behaviors listed here appear to be clear-cut, black-and-white. However, in real life there may be gray areas that make decision-making difficult. One helpful guideline is to examine your motivation. If your primary goal is to benefit yourself, then it is probably *not* a good action to take. Finally, in extreme cases such as war, when someone's life is in danger or you can prevent actual suffering, it may be acceptable to "break" these rules.

Abbreviated Phowa Visualization and Encouragement

We can practice Phowa with our dying loved one, regardless of their religion or beliefs. It is a way to release one's karma (i.e., grasping and clinging habits) to a higher being. It will bring them relief and love as they embark on the next phase of the cycle of life. Feel free to fill in the higher being that best fits the loved one's beliefs.

Abbreviated Phowa Visualization

Let's close our eyes and rest our mind.

Together, let's calm ourselves and relax.

Let's observe our breath for a few moments in its most natural state.

Just observe the air coming in and out of your nostrils.

Or notice the rise and fall of your chest or abdomen.

If you get distracted by noises or thoughts visiting your mind, that is not a problem. As soon as you notice that, just return to observing your breath.

Let's do it together.

[*For a few minutes observe your own breath in the same manner you just read to them. You are both resting your minds in peacefulness.*]

Feel that your most precious God, higher presence, or golden light is in the room.

[NAME OF HIGHER BEING] is here and with you right now.

[NAME OF HIGHER BEING] is present.

[NAME OF HIGHER BEING] loves you.

As you feel [NAME OF HIGHER BEING], your mind calms and you feel their love.

They have been with you all your life, and now they are here to love and support you.

[NAME OF HIGHER BEING] wants you to be at peace and to feel them merge with your heart and mind.

They want you to feel the essence of their being — which is love for all. Their heart and your heart are together.

How lucky we are that they love you and want to be with you for this next phase.

A soft white light is being emitted from their heart, which extends to just above your head. It seeps from the top of your head into your heart like liquid.

Let's feel that white light flowing into your heart now.

[*Pause*]

You are loved and comforted by their beautiful white light in your heart. Allow it to melt inside of you. Allow your heart to melt and merge with [NAME OF HIGHER BEING].

Feel their presence and their white light energy.

Stay with this beautiful feeling for as long as you like.

You and [NAME OF HIGHER BEING] are united with each other.

You love them and they love you. Your hearts are one.

You are home.

They are here to welcome you.

Stay with [NAME OF HIGHER BEING] for as long as you like.

Repeat this visualization whenever you want to.

Encouragement

This text is based on the teachings of the tantric Buddhist Vajra master Guru Padmasambhava, who lived around the eighth or ninth century CE. Since then, it has helped many beings pass in love and peace.

[LOVED ONE'S NAME].

We are now following the natural state of life.

This is how we all pass through.

This is how we all die.

There is no need to feel fear.

This is as natural as the rain or the wind.

You are here with [NAME OF HIGHER BEING].

[NAME OF HIGHER BEING] is here to love you and assure that you will die in peace.

There is no need to fear.

You are surrounded by love.

The past is gone.

There is nothing that was in your past life that you need. Let it all go.

Now is a time for love and peace.

This is the natural state that we all go through.

There is no need to feel fear.

This is as natural as the rain or the wind.

[*Repeat the entire reading and/or just the final line several times.*]

Acknowledgments

We wish to express our great appreciation to those who helped this book come to fruition: Tom Seidman, Khandro Tsering Choeden, Maricruz Gomez, Alberto Garcia, Cynthia Orozco, Elizabeth Levine, Catherine Scrivens, Joe Kulin, Kristen Cashman, and Nick Taylor.

Notes

Chapter 1: What Is Karma?

p. 3   *"When this exists, that comes to be"*: *The Middle Length Discourses of the Buddha: A New Translation of the Majjhima Nikāya*, trans. Bhikkhu Nanamoli, ed. Bhikkhu Bodhi (Boston: Wisdom Publications, 1995), 655.

p. 5   *"Peace does not come through prayer"*: Dalai Lama, Twitter, August 17, 2010, https://twitter.com/dalailama /status/21391135306.

p. 5   *"Problems created by human beings"*: Dalai Lama, Twitter, May 16, 2016, https://twitter.com/DalaiLama /status/732141062546821120.

p. 6   *"Before you act, you have freedom"*: Yogoda Satsanga Society of India, Facebook, July 1, 2020, https://www .facebook.com/photo/?fbid=10158049606021293&set =a.10152016378876293.

p. 10   *"I am the owner of my actions"*: "Upajjhatthana Sutta: Subjects for Contemplation," trans. Thanissaro

Bhikkhu, Access to Insight (BCBS Edition), November 30, 2013, https://www.accesstoinsight.org/tipitaka/an/ano5/ano5.057.than.html.

Chapter 5: Karma and Habits Are Synonyms?

p. 34   *"All those who are unhappy in the world"*: Shantideva, *A Guide to the Bodhisattva Way of Life (Bodhicaryavatara)*, trans. Vesna A. Wallace and B. Alan Wallace (Ithaca, NY: Snow Lion Publications, 1997), 105, https://thuvienhoasen.org/images/file/EUaZhZ1GoQgQANVp/shantideva-bodhicaryavatara-wallace.pdf.

Chapter 6: How Do You Start Creating Positive Karma?

p. 38   *Mind precedes all mental states*: The Dhammapada: *The Buddha's Path of Wisdom*, trans. Buddharakkhita Thera (Kandy, Sri Lanka: Buddhist Publication Society, 2007), 21.

p. 43   *"What do you think, Rahula: What is a mirror for?"*: "Ambalatthika-rahulovada Sutta: Instructions to Rahula at Mango Stone," trans. Thanissaro Bhikkhu, Access to Insight (BCBS Edition), November 30, 2013, https://www.accesstoinsight.org/tipitaka/mn/mn.061.than.html.

p. 44   *"If, on reflection, you know that it led to self-affliction"*: "Ambalatthika-rahulovada Sutta."

p. 45   *"He who harms living beings is"*: "Dhammapada Verse
270: Balisika Vatthu," trans. Daw Mya Tin, ed. Burma
Tipitaka Association, 1986, https://www.tipitaka.net
/tipitaka/dhp/verseload.php?verse=270. *Ariya* refers to
someone who has reached an elevated level of spiritual
development.

p. 46   *"May all beings have happiness"*: Quoted in Judith
Pickering, *The Search for Meaning in Psychotherapy:
Spiritual Practice, the Apophatic Way, and Bion* (New
York: Routledge, 2019).

p. 48   *"It is spoken at the right time"*: "Vaca Sutta: A State-
ment," trans. Thanissaro Bhikkhu, Access to Insight
(BCBS Edition), July 3, 2010, https://www.access
toinsight.org/tipitaka/an/an05/an05.198.than.html.

p. 48   *"In the case of words that the [Buddha] knows to be
unfactual"*: "Abhaya Sutta: To Prince Abhaya (on Right
Speech)," trans. Thanissaro Bhikkhu, Access to Insight
(BCBS Edition), November 30, 2013, https://www
.accesstoinsight.org/tipitaka/mn/mn.058.than.html.

p. 49   *"When one intends to move or when one intends to
speak"*: Shantideva, *A Guide to the Bodhisattva Way of
Life (Bodhicaryavatara)*, trans. Vesna A. Wallace and
B. Alan Wallace (Ithaca, NY: Snow Lion Publications,
1997), 51, https://thuvienhoasen.org/images/file/EU
aZhZ1GoQgQANVp/shantideva-bodhicaryavatara
-wallace.pdf.

Chapter 10: What If I Don't Believe in Rebirth?

p. 68   *"The moment I die / I will try to come back to you"*: Thich Nhat Hanh, *Call Me by My True Names: The Collected Poems of Thich Nhat Hanh* (Berkeley, CA: Parallax Press, 1993).

p. 68   *"Do not stand / By my grave, and weep"*: Clare Harner, "Immortality," *The Gypsy*, December 1934.

Chapter 12: What's Karma Got to Do with It?

p. 76   *"Where would there be leather enough"*: Shantideva, *A Guide to the Bodhisattva Way of Life (Bodhicaryavatara)*, trans. Vesna A. Wallace and B. Alan Wallace (Ithaca, NY: Snow Lion Publications, 1997), 48, https://thuvien hoasen.org/images/file/EUaZhZ1GoQgQANVp /shantideva-bodhicaryavatara-wallace.pdf.

About the Authors

Venerable **Lama Lhanang Rinpoche** was born in Golok, Amdo, in the northeast of Tibet. As a child, he entered the Thubten Chokor Ling Monastery in the Gande region, Golok, under the guidance of his root teacher Kyabye Orgyen Kusum Lingpa, where in addition to developing a complete monastic education he trained in the yogi lineage of Anu Yoga.

He was recognized as the rebirth of Ken Rinpoche Damcho, an emanation of Nubchen Namke Nyingpo — one of the twenty-five disciples of Guru Rinpoche — by the Sang Long Monastery in eastern Tibet. He has received teachings from many teachers from the different schools and lineages of Tibetan Buddhism, such as His Holiness the Fourteenth Dalai Lama, His Holiness the Fourth Dodruchen Rinpoche, and His Holiness the Fourth Kathok Getse Rinpoche, among others.

Lama Lhanang Rinpoche is a teacher of Vajrayana Buddhism, from the Nyingma school of the Longchen Nyingthig lineage. In addition to Buddhism, he studied history, astrology, grammar, Tibetan medicine, painting, sculpture, music, and theater. All this has led him to share teachings on the proper use of the body, the word, and the mind with the motto "world peace through inner peace." His life in the West has also been dedicated to sharing the teachings of the Buddha through his painting, in which he reflects his relationship with everyday life, no matter where he is in the world.

He is the coauthor of *The Tibetan Book of the Dead for Beginners* and currently lives in San Diego with his wife and child. He directs the Jigme Lingpa Center in addition to sharing his teachings in centers across North America and Europe.

Mordy Levine earned a BA from Brandeis University and an MBA from the University of Chicago Booth School of Business. He is the creator of the Meditation Pro Series, which teaches meditation for different conditions that affect Western civilization (e.g., stress, insomnia, weight issues, and smoking). To date, more than 950,000 people have learned to meditate through his series of meditation programs.

Mordy is the president of Jigme Lingpa Center, a nonprofit organization led by Lama Lhanang Rinpoche. The center's goal is to generate benefit to all beings through the dissemination of the Buddha's teachings of wisdom and compassion, thereby achieving a sustainable future of peace and harmony for all.

He has been practicing yoga and martial arts for forty years. Mordy also holds instructor certifications in karate, tai chi, and yoga.

The coauthor of *The Tibetan Book of the Dead for Beginners*, he lives in Rancho Santa Fe, California, with his wife Elizabeth, their son, and their many dogs.

NEW WORLD LIBRARY is dedicated to publishing books and other media that inspire and challenge us to improve the quality of our lives and the world.

We are a socially and environmentally aware company. We recognize that we have an ethical responsibility to our readers, our authors, our staff members, and our planet.

We serve our readers by creating the finest publications possible on personal growth, creativity, spirituality, wellness, and other areas of emerging importance. We serve our authors by working with them to produce and promote quality books that reach a wide audience. We serve New World Library employees with generous benefits, significant profit sharing, and constant encouragement to pursue their most expansive dreams.

We print our books with soy-based ink on paper from sustainably managed forests. We power our Northern California office with solar energy, and we respectfully acknowledge that it is located on the ancestral lands of the Coast Miwok Indians. We also contribute to nonprofit organizations working to make the world a better place for us all.

Our products are available wherever books are sold.

customerservice@NewWorldLibrary.com
Phone: 415-884-2100 or 800-972-6657
Orders: Ext. 110
Fax: 415-884-2199
NewWorldLibrary.com

Scan below to access our newsletter
and learn more about our books and authors.